ANIMAL ALBUMS
THE BUTTERFLY & MOTH FAMILY
BY GOLRIZ GOLKAR
eureka!
REKA!, AN IMPRINT OF BELLWETHER MEDIA BY FLUTTERBEE

Eureka! books turn real stories into unforgettable experiences. Clear, direct language and sharp, captivating imagery make it easy to follow your curiosity, one fascinating fact at a time.
Your Eureka! moment awaits!

This edition first published in 2027 by Bellwether Media, Inc.

For information regarding permission, write to Bellwether Media, Inc., Attention: Permissions Department, 3500 American Blvd W, Suite 150, Bloomington, MN 55431.

Names: Golkar, Golriz author
Title: The butterfly and moth family / By Golriz Golkar.
Description: Eureka. | Minneapolis, Minnesota : Bellwether Media, Inc, 2027. | Series: Animal albums | Includes index. | Audience: Ages 9-13 | Audience: Grades 7-9 | Summary: "Engaging images accompany information on butterflies and moths. The text level and subject matter are intended for students in grades 5 through 9" Provided by publisher.
Identifiers: LCCN 2026010704 (print) | LCCN 2026010705 (ebook) | ISBN 9798898801328 (library binding) | ISBN 9798898802561 (ebook)
Subjects: LCSH: Butterflies | Moths | Lepidoptera--Behavior | LCGFT: juvenile literature
Classification: LCC QL544.2 .G655 2027 (print) | LCC QL544.2 (ebook) | DDC 595.78/9--dc23/eng/20260224
LC record available at https://lccn.loc.gov/2026010704
LC ebook record available at https://lccn.loc.gov/2026010705

Editor: Rebecca Sabelko Series Designer: Jeff Kollock

Printed in the United States of America, North Mankato, MN.

TABLE OF CONTENTS

WHAT ARE BUTTERFLIES AND MOTHS?

Butterflies and moths are insects in the Lepidoptera order. There are around 180,000 species of butterflies and moths. They live on all continents except Antarctica. They are found in nearly all land habitats. Most butterflies are active during the day. Moths are usually active at night.

▲ POLYPHEMUS MOTH

KINGDOM
ANIMALIA

PHYLUM
ARTHROPODA

CLASS
INSECTA

ORDER
LEPIDOPTERA

TAXONOMY CHART

Butterflies and moths vary in appearance and behavior. But they share many similarities. They are both covered in scales. The scales on their wings take in and reflect light. This creates different colors and patterns. The insects are important pollinators that undergo a complete metamorphosis.

COCOON▼

GOLDEN BIRDWING BUTTERFLY▲
after metamorphosis

DELICATE SCALES

The scales on butterflies and moths rub off easily when handled. Their wings are easily damaged too. It is best to avoid touching them.

THE HISTORY OF BUTTERFLIES AND MOTHS

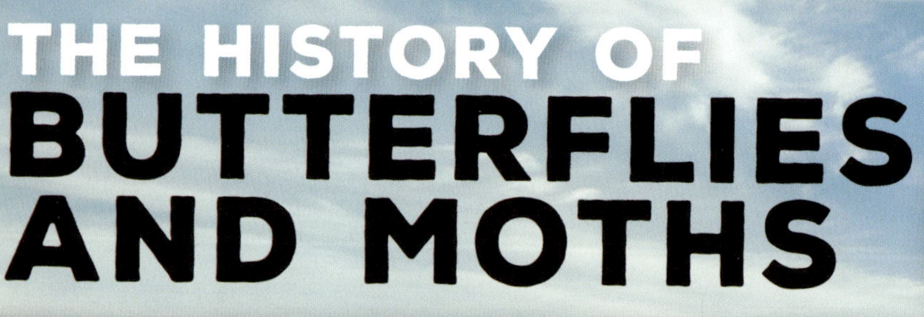

The first moths appeared on Earth about 300 million years ago. Moths evolved their hearing many times. Some became able to hear ultrasonic sound. This helped them better escape bats.

Moths developed feeding tubes called proboscises around 241 million years ago. They likely used these to drink energy-rich foods like sap. Moths became more diverse after flowering plants evolved. Some moths started drinking flower nectar during the day around 100 million years ago. These moths evolved into butterflies. Their colors and patterns changed over time as they adapted to different habitats.

EVOLUTIONARY EXCELLENCE

ANTENNAE
help butterflies and moths smell and balance while flying

SCALES
help butterflies and moths camouflage, warn predators, attract mates, regulate temperature, and fly

EARLIKE STRUCTURES
help butterflies and moths hear ultrasonic sound

PROBOSCIS
helps butterflies and moths eat nectar and other liquids

LIFE CYCLE

Butterflies and moths go through a four-stage metamorphosis. Females lay hundreds to more than one thousand eggs on or near host plants. The eggs hatch when the weather and host plant growth are just right. Larvae, or caterpillars, eat large amounts of their host plants for several weeks. Caterpillars shed their skin several times as they grow. This is called molting.

MOTH ▲
laying eggs

MOTH PUPA ▼
inside a cocoon

MOTH CATERPILLAR ▶

MOLTING ▼

Grown caterpillars become pupae. Many moths spin silk cocoons around themselves. Most butterflies form hard chrysalises. Insects rebuild their body parts during this stage. They come out as adult moths or butterflies.

BUTTERFLY ▲
coming out of its chrysalis

LIFE SPANS

GIANT SWALLOWTAIL BUTTERFLY

2 WEEKS

MONARCH BUTTERFLY

6 WEEKS

POLYPHEMUS MOTH

4 DAYS

LUNA MOTH

7 DAYS

BUTTERFLY AND MOTH LANGUAGE AND BEHAVIOR

BEHAVIORS

Many moths and butterflies migrate to find warmer weather. Some migrate in a single generation. But most do not finish the entire migration by themselves. It can take up to five generations to complete a migration.

Butterflies and moths are active at different times. Butterflies mostly use sight to find flowers during the day. Most moths use scent to find food at night.

COMMUNICATION

Butterflies and moths may use their colors and patterns to scare off predators. Color and pattern also help them defend their territories. Their colors help them attract mates too. Both males and females also use chemicals to show they are ready to mate.

GOLDEN EMPEROR MOTH ▲

NOISY INSECTS

Gossamer-winged butterflies make clicking sounds with their wings to attract ants. Ants help protect the butterflies. Other butterfly species make squeaking or grating sounds to ward off predators.

BUTTERFLY AND MOTH FAMILY TREE

BUTTERFLIES

Many scientists agree there are six families of butterflies. One of these families includes skippers.

▲**BRUSH-FOOTED BUTTERFLIES**
over 7,200 species
MONARCH BUTTERFLIES

WHITE, SULPHUR, JEZEBEL, AND CABBAGE BUTTERFLIES▲
around 1,100 species
CLOUDLESS SULPHUR BUTTERFLIES

▲**SWALLOWTAIL BUTTERFLIES**
around 600 species
GIANT SWALLOWTAIL BUTTERFLIES

▲**HAIRSTREAK, BLUE, AND COPPER BUTTERFLIES**
around 5,000 species
GREAT PURPLE HAIRSTREAK BUTTERFLIES

METALMARK BUTTERFLIES▲
around 1,300 species
DUKE OF BURGUNDY BUTTERFLIES

LEPIDOPTERA

MOTHS

There are around 125 moth families.

▲ **GIANT SILK MOTHS**
more than 1,000 species
LUNA MOTHS

▲ **TIGER MOTHS**
around 11,000 species
GIANT LEOPARD MOTHS

▲ **SPHINX MOTHS**
over 1,400 species
HUMMINGBIRD HAWK MOTHS

▲ **PLUME MOTHS**
more than 1,500 species
COMMON PLUME MOTHS

GEOMETER MOTHS ▲
around 24,000 species
COMMON EMERALD MOTHS

MONARCH BUTTERFLIES

Monarch butterflies complete a two-way migration over multiple generations. They travel up to 3,000 miles (4,828 kilometers).

WHERE DO THEY LIVE?

Monarchs mostly live in North America. Some live in parts of Europe and Oceania. Monarchs are found where milkweed grows during the breeding season.

DIET

Caterpillars eat milkweed plants. These plants contain toxins that make the butterflies poisonous to predators. Adults drink nectar from many flowers.

▲CHRYSALIS

CATERPILLAR▲
eating a milkweed plant

WHAT'S THAT SMELL?

The black spots on male monarchs' wings are scent glands. They help males attract females.

APPEARANCE

Adults have bright orange wings with black veins. Small white dots line the edges. Males are usually bigger than females. They have a black spot on each of their hind wings.

SPECIES PROFILE

VICEROY BUTTERFLY

- **Range:** southern Canada, the U.S., northern Mexico
- **Known for:** Viceroys mimic monarchs. But viceroys have distinct black stripes across their hind wings.

SIZE COMPARISON

4IN (10.2 cm)

monarch butterfly

8IN (20.3 cm)

blue morpho butterfly

2.5IN (6.4 cm)

painted lady butterfly

PAINTED LADY BUTTERFLIES

Painted ladies are among the most widespread butterfly species. Their long migrations take up to 10 generations to complete.

APPEARANCE

Adults' wings are usually pinkish orange with black lines and white spots. Some have shades of blue, brown, pink, and red. Small eyespots are on the duller undersides of their hind wings.

DIET

Caterpillars prefer nettle and thistle plants. Adults are often found drinking nectar from flowers in the aster family.

ADULT drinking nectar from an aster flower

CATERPILLAR on a thistle plant

FLYING FAR

A single painted lady butterfly can cover more than 4,000 miles (6,437 kilometers) during migration.

PAINTED LADY BUTTERFLY
Range in the Wild

WHERE DO THEY LIVE?

Painted ladies are mostly found in parts of Africa, Asia, Europe, and North America. Preferred habitats include fields and grasslands.

SPECIES PROFILE

AMERICAN PAINTED LADY BUTTERFLY

- **Range:** parts of North America to northern South America
- **Known for:** American painted ladies have two large eyespots on their underwings.

SIZE COMPARISON

4IN (10.2 cm)

monarch butterfly

1.65IN (4.2 cm)

great purple hairstreak butterfly

2.5IN (6.4 cm)

painted lady butterfly

BLUE MORPHO BUTTERFLIES

Blue morphos are among the biggest butterflies in the world. Their wingspans are up to 8 inches (20.3 centimeters) wide.

APPEARANCE

Adult males have bright blue wings with black edges. Their undersides are mostly brown with black and yellow eyespots. Cream and orange spots often outline their wings. Females often have less bright coloring.

DIET

Caterpillars mostly eat plants from the pea family. They make the caterpillars poisonous to predators. Adults prefer rotting fruit, tree sap, mud, and the juices of dead animals.

SIZE COMPARISON

3IN (7.6 cm)

cloudless sulphur butterfly

8IN (20.3 cm)

blue morpho butterfly

1.3IN (3.4 cm)

common emerald moth

SPECIES PROFILE

PELEIDES BLUE MORPHO

- **Range:**
  Mexico and Central and South America
- **Known for:**
  They are often found in butterfly houses or rainforest exhibits at museums and zoos in the U.S.

LOOK OUT!

Blue morpho larvae sometimes eat one another. This may be a way to control their populations when there is limited food to eat.

= Range

PELEIDES BLUE MORPHO BUTTERFLY

Range in the Wild

WHERE DO THEY LIVE?

Blue morphos are found in Mexico, Central America, and South America. They live in rainforests and other wooded areas.

CLOUDLESS SULPHUR BUTTERFLIES

Cloudless sulphurs fly much closer to the ground than many other butterfly species.

= Range

CLOUDLESS SULPHUR BUTTERFLY

Range in the Wild

WHERE DO THEY LIVE?

Cloudless sulphurs live in parts of North, Central, and South America. They are often spotted in parks and gardens.

DIET

Caterpillars eat many toxic plants that are dangerous to predators. Adults have long proboscises. These help them drink from flowers that many insects cannot reach.

SPECIES PROFILE

ORANGE SULPHUR BUTTERFLY

Range:
North America, Central America, South America

Known for:
They have pale orange wings with dark edges. These butterflies fly close to the ground over flowering plants such as alfalfa, clover, and sunflowers.

APPEARANCE

Adult males have light yellow wings. Females' wings have a black border. Many have a dark spot in the center of each forewing.

FEMALE

MALE

COLOR CHANGING

Cloudless sulphur caterpillars turn green when they eat leaves. They become yellow when they eat yellow flowers. They blend in with their surroundings!

SIZE COMPARISON

3IN (7.6 cm)
cloudless sulphur butterfly

5.5IN (14 cm)
giant swallowtail butterfly

1.65IN (4.2 cm)
great purple hairstreak butterfly

GIANT SWALLOWTAIL BUTTERFLIES

Giant swallowtails have taillike extensions on their hind wings. They are the largest butterfly species in North America.

DIET

Caterpillars mostly eat citrus plants. Adults drink nectar from flowers such as azaleas and swamp milkweed. They also drink liquids from mud puddles.

SIZE COMPARISON

4IN (10.2 cm)

monarch butterfly

5.5IN (14 cm)

giant swallowtail butterfly

2.3IN (5.7 cm)

silver-spotted skipper

WHERE DO THEY LIVE?

Giant swallowtails are found in Canada, the United States, Mexico, and the Caribbean. Those that live in cold regions migrate for winter. Some overwinter in their chrysalises.

APPEARANCE

Adults have blackish-brown wings with yellow spotted bands. A yellow spot marks the end of each tail. The undersides are yellow with red, black, and blue marks. Their bodies are yellow with a black mark.

SPECIES PROFILE

ZEBRA SWALLOWTAIL BUTTERFLY

- **Range:** U.S. and southeastern Canada
- **Known for:** They have long, triangle-shaped wings with dark zebralike stripes.

GREAT PURPLE HAIRSTREAK BUTTERFLIES

Great purple hairstreaks have black tails and eyelike markings on their hind wings. These create false heads! These butterflies are more likely to escape predators that attack their false heads.

WHERE DO THEY LIVE?

Great purple hairstreaks are mostly found in the southern U.S. and parts of Mexico and Central America. They prefer gardens, woodlands, and swamps.

GREAT PURPLE HAIRSTREAK BUTTERFLY

Range in the Wild

DIET

Caterpillars eat only mistletoe plants. This makes them poisonous to predators. Adults drink nectar from flowers such as zinnias, milkweed, and goldenrod.

APPEARANCE

Adults have shiny blue wings with black borders. Their undersides are purplish black. Their bodies are blue on top and orange on the bottom.

SIZE COMPARISON

1.3IN (3.4 cm)

common emerald moth

4IN (10.2 cm)

monarch butterfly

1.65IN (4.2 cm)

great purple hairstreak butterfly

SPECIES PROFILE

WHITE-LETTER HAIRSTREAK BUTTERFLY

- **Range:** United Kingdom
- **Known for:** These butterflies have brown underwings, orange wing edges, and white, W-shaped streaks on their wings. People rarely see them because they fly around treetops.

DUKE OF
BURGUNDY BUTTERFLIES

Duke of Burgundy butterflies are rarely seen. These butterflies are most active on sunny mornings. They usually stay close to their breeding sites.

WHERE DO THEY LIVE?

Duke of Burgundys are found across much of Europe. They live in grasslands and clearings in woodlands. Pupae may overwinter in chrysalises in thick grasses until spring.

DIET

Duke of Burgundy caterpillars eat the leaves of primrose and cowslip plants at night. Adults drink nectar.

SIZE COMPARISON

1.25IN (3.2 cm)	2.5IN (6.4 cm)	1.3IN (3.4 cm)

Duke of Burgundy butterfly	painted lady butterfly	common emerald moth

SPECIES PROFILE

LITTLE METALMARK BUTTERFLY

- **Range:** eastern U.S.
- **Known for:** Little metalmarks are one of the smallest butterflies. Their wingspan is around 1 inch (2.5 centimeters). Silver markings and dark spots line their light brown to orange wings.

WALKING BUTTERFLIES

Duke of Burgundys are metalmark butterflies. Most male metalmarks only use four of their six legs. Two of their legs are shorter. Females use all six legs to walk.

APPEARANCE

Duke of Burgundys have brown wings with orange markings. White-and-brown fringe outlines their wings. Their underwings are brown and dark orange. White dots the underside of their hind wings.

SILVER-SPOTTED SKIPPERS

Silver-spotted skippers are among the largest and most well-known skipper species.

APPEARANCE

Silver-spotted skippers have brown wings. A band of orange runs through the center of each forewing. Silvery-white markings are found on each hind wing.

WHAT ARE SKIPPERS?

Skippers are butterflies. But they have characteristics of butterflies and moths. They are known for their fast, bouncy way of flying.

DIET

Caterpillars eat the leaves of black and honey locusts, false indigos, and American wisterias. Adults may be found drinking nectar from milkweeds, blazing stars, and thistles.

WHERE DO THEY LIVE?

Silver-spotted skippers are found throughout the U.S. and southern Canada. They live near roadsides and woodlands. They also live in gardens and fields.

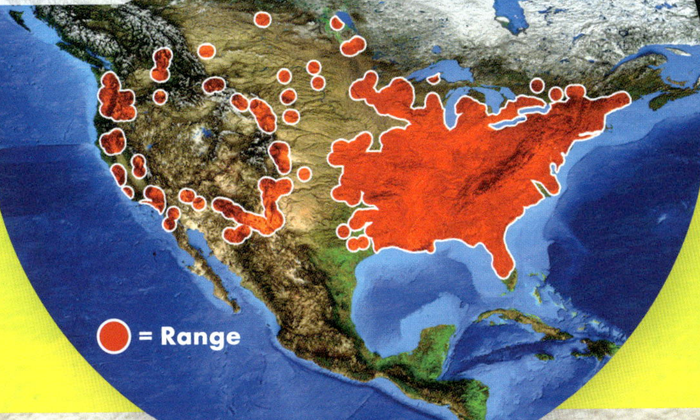

SIZE COMPARISON

6IN (15.2 cm)

Polyphemus moth

8IN (20.3 cm)

blue morpho butterfly

2.3IN (5.7 cm)

silver-spotted skipper

VULNERABLE SPECIES

OTTOE SKIPPER
▼ ENDANGERED ▼

THREATS

habitat loss

heavy animal grazing

controlled fires

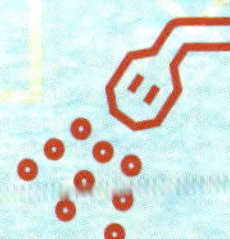

herbicide usage

CONSERVATION EFFORTS ▼

land management

education on the effects of controlled fires on insects

land surveys

LUNA MOTHS

Luna moths are nocturnal silk moths. Like other silk moths, they do not have a mouth or digestive system. They do not eat because they only live for about one week.

DIET

Caterpillars spend around one month eating a lot of leaves. They may eat from walnut, hickory, and birch trees.

TRICKING BATS

Bats are luna moths' main predators. Luna moths use eyespots to confuse bats. They also move their long tails in circles to make it harder for bats to catch them.

SIZE COMPARISON

1.06IN (2.7 cm)

common plume moth

4.5IN (11.4 cm)

luna moth

2.5IN (6.4 cm)

painted lady butterfly

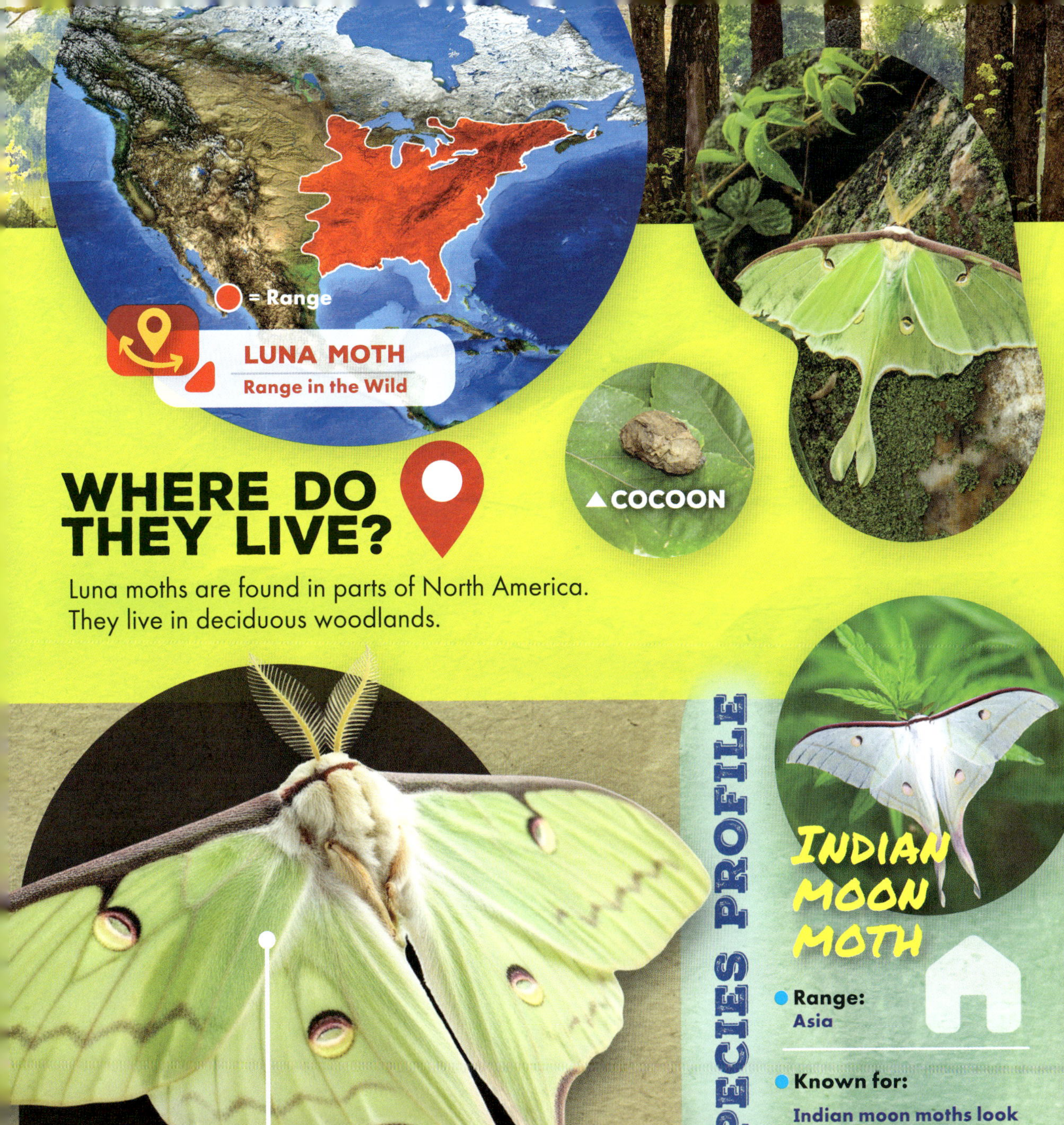

WHERE DO THEY LIVE?

Luna moths are found in parts of North America. They live in deciduous woodlands.

APPEARANCE

Luna moths can be different shades of green. Their wings often have a dark border. Eyespots on each wing help keep predators away. Each hind wing has a long tail.

SPECIES PROFILE

INDIAN MOON MOTH

- **Range:** Asia
- **Known for:** Indian moon moths look quite similar to luna moths. But they are more yellow than green. Their tails often include shades of pink.

GIANT LEOPARD MOTHS

Giant leopard moths are known for the black, leopard-like spots on their wings. These moths are often called tiger moths.

WHERE DO THEY LIVE?

These moths are found from southern Canada to northern South America. Their habitats include woodlands, gardens, riverbanks, and fields.

DIET

Caterpillars eat cabbage, willow, citrus, and sunflower plants. Adults usually do not eat because their lives are very short.

SIZE COMPARISON

3.5IN (8.9 cm)	6IN (15.2 cm)	1.3IN (3.4 cm)
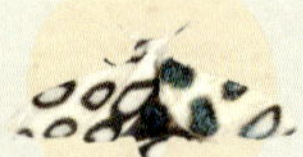		
giant leopard moth	Polyphemus moth	common emerald moth

BAT ALERT

Bats are giant leopard moths' main predators. Earlike parts on the moths' hind wings can hear bats' sound waves. The moths make clicking sounds that break up sound waves. These defenses help keep the moths safe!

APPEARANCE

Giant leopard moths have white wings. Their forewings have black rings. Their bodies have shiny blue, orange, and black markings.

SPECIES PROFILE

SALT MARSH MOTH

- **Range:** North and Central America
- **Known for:** These moths have white forewings with black spots.

POLYPHEMUS MOTHS

Polyphemus moths are large silk moths with striking eyespots. They get their name from a mythological Greek giant with a single large eye on its forehead.

APPEARANCE

These moths have reddish-brown, tan, or brown wings crossed with a dark line. Each forewing has a small yellow eyespot. Each hind wing has an eyespot with a clear center that is outlined in blue, black, and yellow.

SPECIES PROFILE

IMPERIAL MOTH

- **Range:** **U.S., Canada, Mexico**
- **Known for:** **These moths have yellow wings with pink, orange, or purple-brown spots. They blend in with the dried leaves of maple, hickory, and tulip trees.**

COCOON ▶

DIET

Caterpillars eat leaves from birch, oak, and hazelnut trees. Adults survive on energy stored from when they were caterpillars.

SIZE COMPARISON

3.5IN (8.9 cm)	6IN (15.2 cm)	1.06IN (2.7 cm)
giant leopard moth	Polyphemus moth	common plume moth

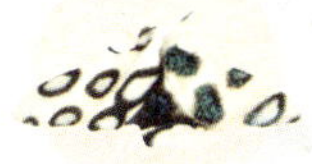

WHERE DO THEY LIVE?

Polyphemus moths live in southern Canada, the U.S., and northern Mexico. Their habitats include wetlands, forests, parks, and orchards.

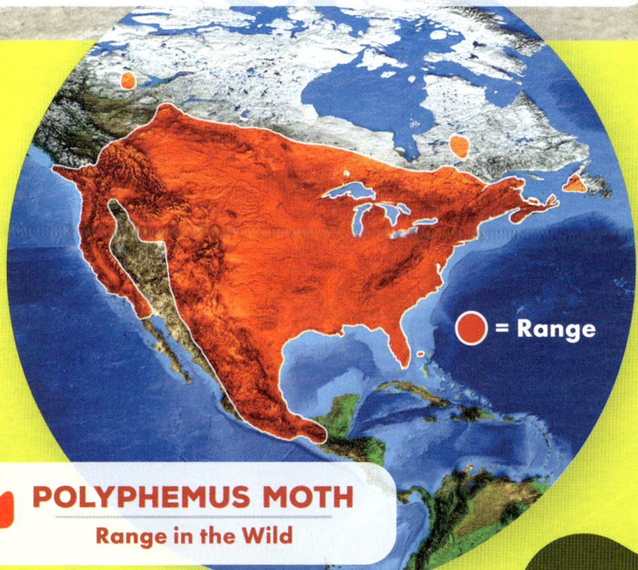

= Range

POLYPHEMUS MOTH
Range in the Wild

HUMMINGBIRD HAWK MOTHS

Hummingbird hawk moths are named for their similarities to hummingbirds. These moths look like they have feathers. They hover near flowers to drink nectar.

HUMMINGBIRD HAWK MOTH
Range in the Wild

WHERE DO THEY LIVE?

Hummingbird hawk moths are found throughout Eurasia and North Africa. They live in many habitats including woodlands, gardens, coastal areas, and cities.

DIET

Caterpillars mostly feed on the leaves of galium plants. Adults are active during the day. They use a long proboscis to drink nectar from flowers such as honeysuckles and red valerians.

SIZE COMPARISON

luna moth	Polyphemus moth	hummingbird hawk moth
4.5IN (11.4 cm)	6IN (15.2 cm)	2.3IN (5.8 cm)

SPECIES PROFILE

HUMMINGBIRD CLEARWING MOTH

- **Range:** North America
- **Known for:** Hummingbird clearwing moths have clear wings with a red-brown border.

APPEARANCE

Hummingbird hawk moths have thick, gray bodies. Their long, black-and-white hairs look like a tail. Their forewings are grayish brown. Their hind wings are bright orange.

COMMON
PLUME MOTHS

Common plume moths are also called morning glory plumes or T-moths. Plume moths have long, narrow bodies. They hold their wings in tight rolls while at rest. This makes them look like the letter T.

DIET

Caterpillars eat many plants. But they are most often found on morning glories. Adults feed on nectar and flower pollen.

SPECIES PROFILE

IRONWEED PLUME MOTH

Range:
U.S. and Canada

Known for:
These moths are white with dark brown heads. They drink nectar from ironweed plants and morning glories.

WHERE DO THEY LIVE?

Common plume moths live on every continent except Australia and Antarctica. They are found in woodlands, scrublands, and gardens.

APPEARANCE

These moths are brown to grayish white. Their feathery forewings are often divided into two plumes. Their hind wings usually have three fringed plumes. They have long, thin legs.

SIZE COMPARISON

3.5IN (8.9 cm)

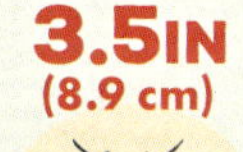

giant leopard moth

2.3IN (5.7 cm)

silver-spotted skipper

1.06IN (2.7 cm)

common plume moth

DRAWN TO THE LIGHT

These moths sometimes rest near lights at night. They also rest on the sides of buildings or fences.

COMMON EMERALD MOTHS

Common emerald moths are most known for their bright green color. Sharp tips on their hind wings are another well-known feature.

APPEARANCE

Common emerald moths are mostly green. Two wavy, pale lines run across their forewings. A checkered fringe outlines their wings.

DIET

Caterpillars eat leaves from many tree species. These include hawthorns, oaks, willows, and birches. Moths drink flower nectar, tree sap, and juices from rotting fruits.

▲ CATERPILLAR

WHERE DO THEY LIVE?

Common emerald moths are mostly found in Eurasia. But there are small populations in areas of North America. They live in woodlands, scrublands, and gardens.

SPECIES PROFILE

WAVY-LINED EMERALD MOTH CATERPILLAR

- **Range:** North America
- **Known for:** These caterpillars are sometimes called camouflaged loopers. They stick bits of plants to their bodies to hide from predators.

SIZE COMPARISON

3.5IN (8.9 cm)

giant leopard moth

4.5IN (11.4 cm)

luna moth

1.3IN (3.4 cm)

common emerald moth

BUTTERFLIES, MOTHS, AND PEOPLE

Butterflies and moths have been important to humans for thousands of years. Many ancient cultures honored them in folktales and myths. They are considered symbols of beauty, rebirth, and the inner spirit. Butterflies and moths are often featured in art, books, and fashion.

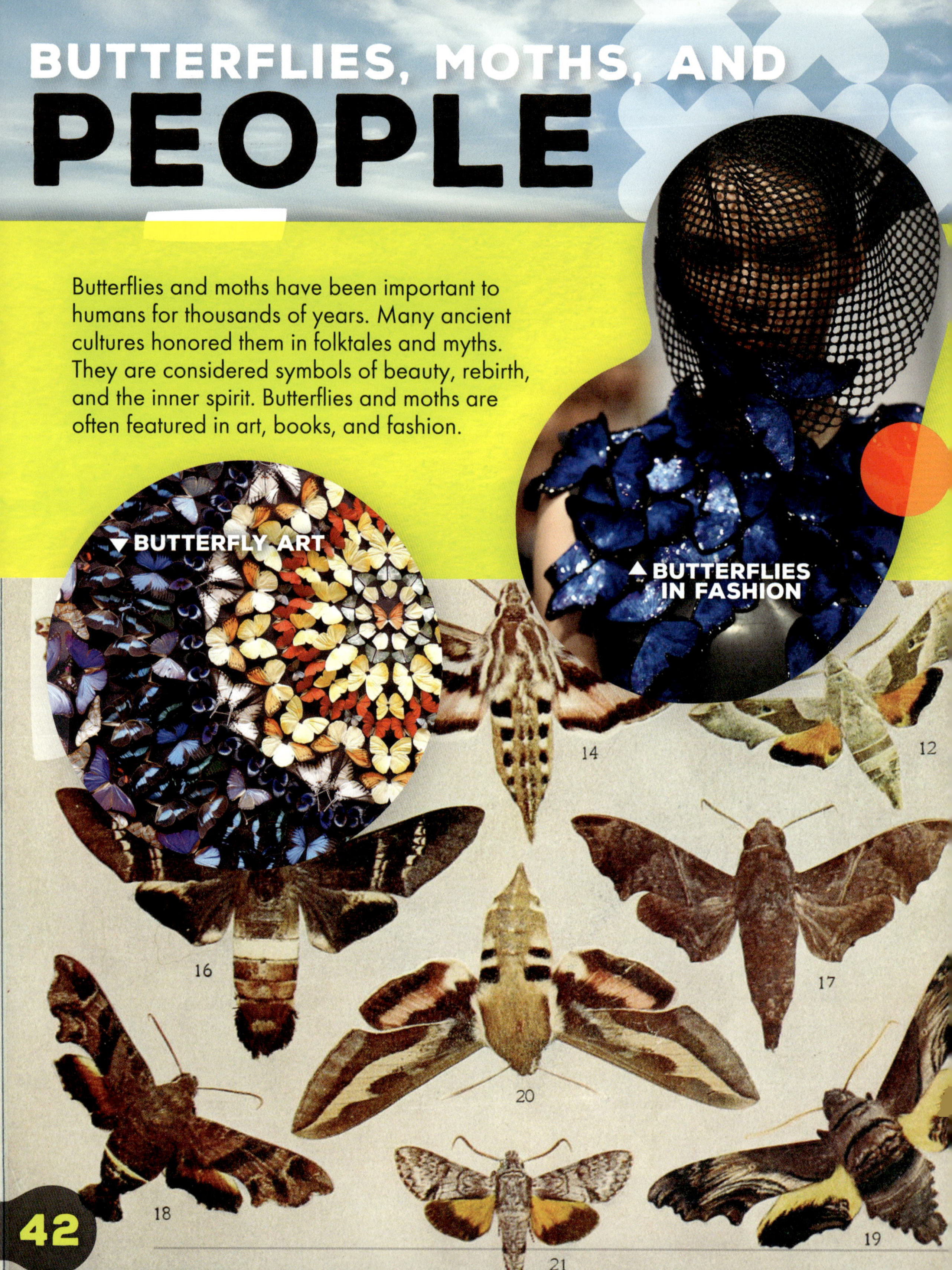

▼ BUTTERFLY ART

▲ BUTTERFLIES IN FASHION

▲LAND DEVELOPMENT

However, these insects are threatened by human behaviors. Land development destroys their habitats and food sources. Climate change, pesticides, and pollution are harming butterflies and moths at all stages of life. Invasive plants and animals overwhelm their food sources and disrupt food webs.

FOLKLORE PROFILE

NAME:

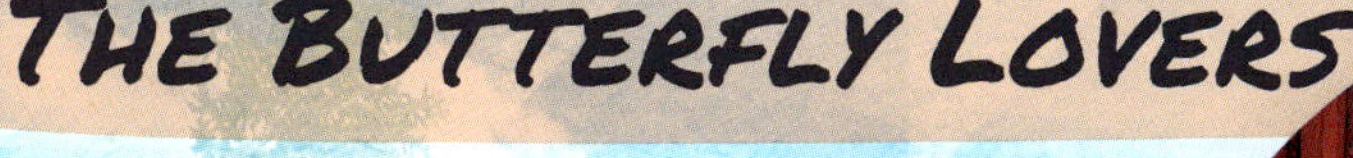

COUNTRY:

CHINA

FAMOUS FOR:

This Chinese folktale tells the story of two lovers who are kept apart by their families. When the lovers die, they turn into butterflies and fly away to live happily together. The butterflies represent love and loyalty.

THE BUTTERFLY LOVERS PERFORMANCE

Butterflies and moths need help to survive. Many organizations work to protect their habitats. Some plant more host plants and work to save land. Others inform the public about the important role butterflies and moths play in keeping habitats healthy.

Slowing climate change is important. Driving less, reducing energy use, and recycling can create less pollution. Planting native species helps keep the air clean. Protecting butterflies and moths today can help keep nature in balance well into the future.

RECYCLING▲

▼NATIVE PLANTS in a pollinator garden

GLOSSARY

adapted—changed over a period of time

climate change—a human-caused process in which Earth's average weather changes over a long period of time

cultures—the beliefs, arts, and ways of life in places or societies

deciduous—related to trees and shrubs with leaves that fall off every year

diverse—made up of animals that are different from one another

Eurasia—a land mass that includes Europe and Asia

evolved—changed from one form into a new form

forewing—one of the two top wings of a butterfly or moth

fringe—fine, closely set hairs or scales on the outer edges of the wings of some butterflies and moths

generation—a group of animals born and living during the same time

habitats—natural homes of plants and animals

hind wings—the bottom wings of a butterfly or moth

invasive—related to an organism that is not native to the place it is found and likely to take over native species and ecosystems

larvae—young insects

metamorphosis—a big change in how some animals look and act, usually related to growing

migrate—to move from one place to another

mythological—related to a collection of stories and ideas from a certain group or culture

native—originally from a certain place

nocturnal—active at night

pesticides—materials that kill pests such as insects or weeds

plumes—long sections of the body

pollinators—animals that spread pollen from one flower to another; pollen is a fine dust that helps plants make seeds.

pollution—substances that make the earth dirty or unsafe; pollution usually comes from humans' actions.

pupae—young insects that are about to become adults

rainforests—thick, green forests that receive a lot of rain

scrublands—dry lands that have mostly low plants and few trees

species—groups of living things that are alike and can reproduce with one another; subspecies are particular types of animals that exist within a species.

threatened—in danger

ultrasonic—related to sound waves that bats and some other animals make; humans cannot hear ultrasonic sounds.

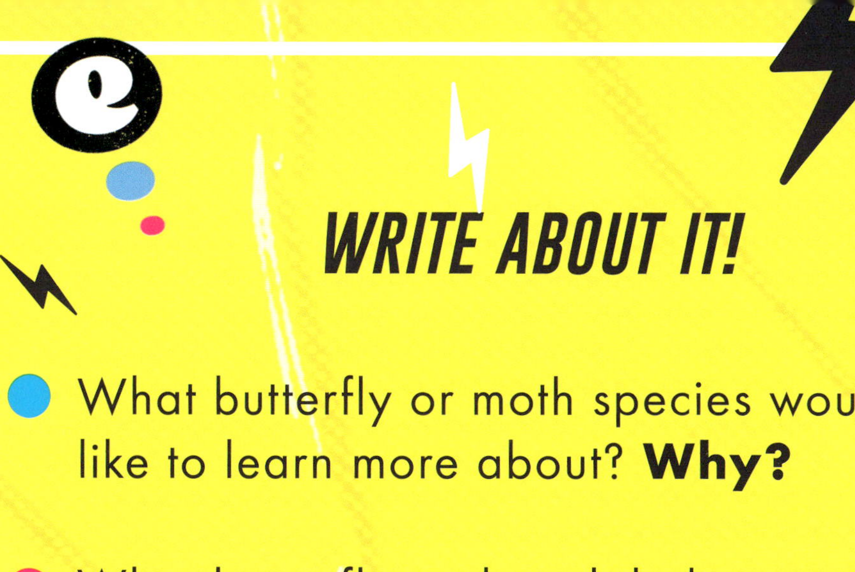

WRITE ABOUT IT!

- What butterfly or moth species would you like to learn more about? **Why?**
- What butterfly and moth behaviors do you think are the most interesting? **Why?**
- **What** changes can you make in your life that could help keep these insects safe?

ALSO CHECK OUT

ANIMAL ALBUMS
THE SNAKE FAMILY
eureka!

ANIMAL ALBUMS
THE CAT FAMILY
eureka!

ANIMAL ALBUMS
THE SHARK FAMILY
eureka!

INDEX

The images in this book are reproduced through the courtesy of: Melinda Fawver, front cover, p. 34 (main); leekris, front cover, pp. 10 (right), 12 (swallowtail), 20 (middle); New Africa, front cover; Michael, front cover; Alvaro, front cover; Ian Luck, front cover; Soho A studio, p. 2; de WS_AK, pp. 3, 11; Niklas, p. 3; amphaiwan, p. 4 (top); avdwolde, p. 4; Dean Pennala, p. 4 (bottom); wisannumkarng, p. 5 (cocoon); Satakorn, p. 5; tomatito26, p. 5 (fun fact); phototrip.cz, p. 6 (top); Chris, pp. 6 (left), 18 (bottom); ondreicka, pp. 6 (right), 13 (leopard), 30 (bottom); Huang, p. 6 (bottom); Leon, p. 7 (top); Nagel Photography, p. 7 (left); Valeriy Kirsanov, p. 7 (right); puteli, p. 8 (top); N_Doerge, p. 8 (left); Tomasz Keljdysz, p. 8 (right); pimmimemom, pp. 8 (molt), 22 (main); Leena Robinson, pp. 9, 22 (right); erry B, p. 9 (swallowtail); Eric, p. 9 (monarch); Kevin Collison, p. 9 (Polyphemus); Danita Delimont, p. 9 (luna); gudkovandrey, p. 10 (top); Miguel, p. 10 (left); Ilshat, p. 10 (bottom); Okeksii, p. 11 (top); gnagel, p. 11 (right); Alen thien, p. 11 (bottom); Rainer Fuhrmann, p. 11 (fun fact); mramsdell1967, p. 12 (monarch); Chase D'Animulls, pp. 12 (sulphur), 24 (main), 35 (bottom); Jim, pp. 12 (purple), 23; Stephan Morris, pp. 12 (Duke), 26 (top), 27; KQ Ferris, p. 13 (luna); Frank, p. 13 (hawk); Sandra Standbridge, pp. 13 (plume), 38 (top); Tony Tilford, p. 13 (emerald); JHVEPhoto, p. 14 (top); Dave, p. 14 (chrysalis); Nicholas J. Klein, p. 14 (left); Nina, p. 14 (right); Georges, p. 15 (profile); thawats, pp. 15 (main), 45 (moth); Alexander, p. 16 (top); Maros, p. 16 (main); Oasishifi, p. 16 (left); jbosvert, p. 16 (right); alinamd, p. 17; samray, p. 17 (profile); papadomus, p. 17 (bottom); Armando Maynez/ Wikimedia Commons, p. 18 (top); Diego Delso/ Wikimedia Commons, p. 18 (left); Michael Gray, p. 18 (main); Michael Garlick/ Wikimedia Commons, p. 18 (middle); Marco, p. 18 (leaf); Wirestock Creators, p. 19; Luca love photo, p. 19 (profile); Melissa McMasters/ Wikimedia Commons, p. 20 (top); sheilaf2002, p. 20 (left); Donna Bollenbach, p. 20 (right); Riverwalker, p. 21 (profile); Samuel, pp. 21 (top), 25 (left); Lena, p. 21 (main); NA, p. 21 (fun fact); S L Jordan Images, p. 21; Lin, p. 22 (top); Diane C Macdonald, p. 22 (left); Darell Gulin/Danita Delimont, p. 23 (profile); Leila Dasher/ Wikimedia Commons, p. 24 (top); Katja Schulz/ Wikimedia Commons, p. 24 (left); cricketsblog/ Wikimedia Commons, pp. 24 (bottom), 25 (top, right); jnakev, p. 25 (profile); Marin, p. 26 (left); blickwinkel/ Alamy, p. 26 (right); Smudge 9000/ Wikimedia Commons, p. 26 (bottom); Judy Gallagher/ Wikimedia Commons, p. 27 (profile); Charles J. Sharp/ Wikimedia Commons, p. 27 (fun fact); José Luis Sánchez Ma, p. 27 (main); PR Photos, p. 28 (top); Mark, p. 28 (middle); YK, p. 28 (bottom); chas53, p. 28 (main); Brandon Olafsson, p. 29 (top); Antony Ratcliffe/ Alamy, p. 29 (middle); andybirkey, p. 29 (bottom); Michael Redmer, p. 30 (top); Ivan Kuzmin, p. 30 (left); Hamilton, p. 30 (middle); ondrejprosicky, p. 30 (fun fact); Jay Ondreicka, pp. 31, 32 (top); SailingAway, p. 31 (cocoon); Marigold, p. 31 (main); chamnan phanthong, p. 31 (profile); Moab Republic, p. 32 (middle); Universal Images Group North America LLC/ Alamy, p. 32 (bottom); nawin, p. 33 (top, bottom); Andy Reago & Chrissy McClarren/ Wikimedia Commons, p. 33 (middle, main); Brett, p. 33 (profile); Cathy Keifer, p. 34 (top); Rod Gardner, p. 34 (profile); Stephen Lody Photography/ Wikimedia Commons, p. 34 (bottom); Nancy J. Ondra, p. 35 (cocoon); Mirek Kijewski, p. 35 (top); David, p. 35 (middle); Daniel Dunca, p. 36 (top); Aggi Schmid, p. 36 (left); Christian Musat, p. 36 (right); Larry Dallaire, p. 37 (profile); Margarita, p. 37 (left); Ian Grainger pp. 37 (right), 39; Nolan, p. 37 (main); Holger Uwe Schmitt, Wikimedia Commons, p. 37 (bottom); Dark Egg, p. 38 (left); almacron, p. 38 (right); Wildwatertv, p. 28 (middle); Dave Harrison-Ward, p. 38 (bottom); Muddy knees, p. 39 (main); muhamad mizan bin ngateni, p. 40 (top); Nature Picture Library/ Alamy, pp. 40 (middle), 41 (profile); Larry Doherty, Alamy, p. 40 (bottom); zagorskid, p. 40 (main); IanRedding, p. 41 (top); Barry, p. 41; NHNHNHNH, p. 42 (art); Alexander Koerner/ Getty Images, p. 42 (fashion); Holland, W. J./ Wikimedia Commons, p. 42; tamas, p. 43 (land); licvin, p. 43 (spray); Santiago Felipe/ Getty Images, p. 43 (performance); Andrijko Z./ Wikimedia Commons, p. 43 (statue); Gan, p. 43 (butterflies); edojob, p. 44 (top); Sean Gallup/ Getty Images, p. 44 (middle); StockMediaSeller, p. 44 (left); teptong, p. 44 (right); mladen antonov/ Getty Images, p. 45 (top); Svitlana, p. 45 (recycling); afrin5, p. 45 (middle); Molly Shannon, p. 45 (garden).